SHATTERED

*Journaling Through the
Pain for Healing*

Shamika White-Jefferson

Scripture quotations marked NIV are taken from The Holy Bible, New International Version®, NIV® Copyright © 1973, 1978, 1984, 2011 by Biblica, Inc.® Used by permission. All rights reserved worldwide.

Scripture quotations marked NKJV are taken from the New King James Version®. Copyright © 1982 by Thomas Nelson. Used by permission. All rights reserved.

Scripture quotations marked MSG are taken from THE MESSAGE, copyright © 1993, 2002, 2018 by Eugene H. Peterson. Used by permission of NavPress. All rights reserved. Represented by Tyndale House Publishers, Inc.

Scripture quotations marked NLT are taken from the Holy Bible, New Living Translation, copyright © 1996, 2004, 2015 by Tyndale House Foundation. Used by permission of Tyndale House Publishers, Inc., Carol Stream, Illinois 60188. All rights reserved.

Cover designed by GermanCreative

Printed in the United States of America
First Printing: January 2021
The Scribe Tribe Publishing Group

THE SCRIBE TRIBE

ISBN-13 978-1-7362882-0-7

I dedicate this book to my husband, Eric Jefferson Jr. and our boys, Deovion and Eric Jefferson III. In all of you, I have found everything that I didn't realize that I needed. You all complete me, and you are my inspirations on earth for greater and bigger. You prompt my desire for more and I'm grateful that you give me all you have to give. Your love, your smiles and your dreams motivate me to give more and I value all that you bring to my life. Being a wife and a mother is a gift from God and I thank God that He saw greater for me than I saw for myself by giving me each of you. I pray my journey helps you on your way and that knowing my story will give you hope and strength. And most importantly, I pray that my story motivates you to never give up and to trust in God. Amen

ACKNOWLEDGEMENTS

To my mom, Michelle Pikes: You are my strength. Your unwavering strength and faithfulness to God has been my greatest motivation and I want to say, thank you. There are many days that you could have given up, but you didn't. You stayed the course, and you gave the best you had for my brother and I and I really appreciate that. From you, I learned strength, perseverance, hard work and FAITH! I thank God for you, and I pray God gives you double for your trouble!

To my lil' brother, Matthew White III: I love you and I am proud of you. I hope that you never give up on your dreams and I pray I've done something to motivate you. I pray God continues to cover and protect you from danger seen and unseen. Love you and thanks for keeping me on my toes.

To my best friends, Alexis Williams, and Akita Kimber: You women are the best and I thank God for you all. When I didn't have food to eat, Alexis, you fed me. When I didn't have a place to stay, Alexis, you provided me with shelter. When I didn't have anyone to talk to, Kita, you were there. And when I wanted to know more about being a wife, Kita, you schooled me. When it comes to parenting, I watched how both of you sacrificed for your kids and I am forever grateful for you two. I pray that all you two have done for me that God blesses you more abundantly. I love y'all so much. Thank you.

To my best friends/sisters Tamika Pickett and Melanie Pearson: Words can't describe the love I have for you. Thank you both for being the light in the midst of darkness. Thank y'all for putting up with me and my southside ways. LOL! Thank you both for showing me how to relax and enjoy life. It brings me great pleasure to acknowledge the love and support that you two bring me and I'm thankful that we are doing this thing called life together. Girls trip after this!

To my male best friend Davon Robb: Thank you for never leaving my side even when I was walking in darkness. God granted you access to me during my pit experience and I thank God that He allowed you to see me. Many noticed but you didn't allow me to stay there. I am forever grateful that no matter what the people had to say about me, you only believed the report of the Lord and that brings me much joy to know that I have you in my corner. Thank you very much and I pray God grants you the desires of your heart. I want you to know that you will be a great husband because you are a great friend. Love ya!

To my best friend/brother, Cedrick Victor: You have shown me what being a friend truly is. Some may never understand the survival skills one has to possess while serving in the military, but you do, and I must say that I would have not survived if it wasn't for God using you. You watched God transform me from the inside out. You saw my struggles and my shortcomings and you still loved me. Thank you for providing me with shelter when I didn't have a place to rest and thank you for being up with me when I cried all night long. Your continued support no matter what city or country you were in gives me great pleasure to call you my friend and brother. Thank you for never giving up because when I see you, I see strength. I love you always.

To my church family: V12, Lifegroup, and Mother Nichols' prayer line. Thank you all so much for your continued prayers and our life conversations. You all have no idea how these groups helped me alone the way. Mother Nichols, thank you for your relationship with God! I pray God continues to provide for you like you provide for others. Chelise, Janise, Emiko, Ebony, Judith, Shaunta, Dion, Gina, Matthew, Vanessa, Estelle, Clarissa, Anna, Angie, Dave, O'Neal and everyone else in my life group, HUGE THANK YOU! I pray everyone can get surrounded by individuals like all of you! Love y'all much!

To my battle buddies, Jeanette, and Holly: Thank you both for everything. I love y'all more than you know. Thanks for listening to me and always being there when I needed you.

To the CEO of my publishing company, Kristen R. Harris: Eyes have not seen nor ears have heard, neither has it entered into the hearts of man what God has in store for you. Every time I think of this scripture, I think of you! Thank you for being a role model and a friend. You have shown everyone you have come into contact with what perseverance looks like and I'm grateful to know you. Thank you for motivating me and keeping me on track with these dates. I appreciate your work ethic and your genuine love. Love you so very much!

To my New Life Covenant SE Pastors: Thank you both so much. It's too many sheep for you all to know me, but the sheep know their Shepherds. I just want you to know that your labor is not in vain. A lot of my skills come from your sermons and a lot of reasons why I didn't give up is because of what and who I was listening to. It is because of you that I joined V12 and the Lifegroup and I want to say, thank you! I pray that everything you all have poured out, be poured back into you, 10 times better. In Jesus' Name, Amen.

To my earthly father: I love you more than words can describe. I hope I make you proud.

And to my Father in Heaven: Thank you for never given up on me and never forsaking me. Amen.

INTRODUCTION

shat·tered

/ˈSHadərd/

adjective

–broken into many pieces

– (of something abstract) damaged or destroyed

–to break (something) into pieces, as by a blow

Shattered is a book designed to reach those whose dreams have been shattered, whose goals have been destroyed, and for those who have been broken by relationships. If you have experienced any of the things I have experienced, you are probably thinking, "I'm broken and destroyed; I am shattered and I have no idea how to put the pieces back together."

If that is you, I'm so happy you picked this book up because I have a secret to share! You are right! You can't fix you alone, but God specializes in broken pieces. He is closer to the broken hearted (Psalm 34:18) and He loves to take the things the world says is damaged goods and do a complete makeover. Our God is the same God yesterday, today, and forever more. (Hebrews 13:8)

During this 21-day devotional, my hope is that while you are journaling, your dreams will be restored, your life will be transformed, and your spirit will be renewed. The word says, "We overcome him by the blood of the lamb and by the words of our testimony." (Revelation 12:11) There is nothing new under the sun. (Ecclesiastes 1:9) So, we decree and declare that the words of our testimony will free and deliver you in the name of Jesus. The word says when you decree a thing, it shall be established unto thee. (Job 22:28)

Remember, the SAME God that did it for Joseph, David, Abraham, Ruth, and even Shamika, will do it for you! He is no respecter of person. (Romans 2:11) Now do yourself a favor; make the above sentence personal.

"The SAME GOD that did it for Joseph, David, Abraham, Ruth, and Shamika will do it for _____!" (Insert your name.) Hallelujah! SAME GOD!

Now, let the journaling begin!

DAY 1

INNER ME

"Although I want to do good, evil is right there with me. For in my inner being I delight in God's law; but I see another law at work in me, waging war against the law of my mind and making me a prisoner of the law of sin at work within me." Romans 7:21b-23

"What a wretched man I am," Paul proclaimed as he admits his faults. Are we like Paul? We battle with the enemy that is really the *inner me*. We make decisions based on our flesh and the result is an epic failure. Do not get me wrong; you must take risks or a leap of faith, but after some moves you must ask yourself, "Was it worth all this pain?

Oh, what a wretched man I am! Or should I say, "Oh, what a wretched woman I am?" Either way, the first step to healing is to admit your faults. Stop right now, look in the mirror and repeat these words. *Oh, what a wretched man/woman I am!* But do not stay there. Get help! And watch God move!

You see, history is designed so that we do not repeat what was already written, but the greatest part of history is that the answer is right before us. According to Google, the average amount of remotely conscious decisions an adult makes each day equals about 35,000, while young children only make about 3,000. So, today let us make every conscious decision count. Everything we ultimately do is based on one decision. The decision on who to date or where to move or what job to take is ultimately your choice to make. Just remember, do not do anything that you will regret later. I believe that if you pray before you move, God will give you exactly what you need. Today, decide to change and pray!

Journal Day 1

Look back over the last year. What are some of the bad decisions that you made? Ask yourself, "Did I pray about this or did I make this decision on my own? How can I get back on track?"

Step 1: Take a few days and write down those decisions that cost you. I'm talking about those decisions that cost your marriage, your job, your car, your home, your freedom, and/or for some that decision that cost you the rights to your children. Think of the heavy things that changed your life. Yep, those right there that you are thinking about. Write those down.

Step 2: Take a few more days and design a plan that can get you back on track.

Example: Set up a day and time when you can apologize to those you hurt. Reconciliation is not for them, but it is a part of your healing plan and you must make things right. Another example could be fixing your credit. Get on the phone and get a copy of your credit report and start checking them off one by one. You got this! You can do it! Just believe in yourself! The best part about life is that if you have breath in your body, God has given you grace to try again.

So...
TRY AGAIN!

DAY 2

FRIENEMIES

This isn't the neighborhood bully mocking me-I could take that. This isn't a foreign devil spitting invective-I could tune that out. It's you! We grew up together! You! My best friend! And this, my best friend, betrayed his best friends; his life betrayed his word. All my life I've been charmed by his speech, never dreaming he'd turn on me. His words, which were music to my ears, turned to daggers in my heart. Psalm 55:12-13, 20-21 MSG

Friends! How many of us have them? A friend is a person who has a strong liking for and trust in another person. Webster dictionary explains that a friend is a person who is not an enemy. So how does one become a frienemy--a friend and enemy. In the beginning of 2018, I listened to a wise man teach on different seats. He explained that sometimes we put the wrong people in the wrong seats. Perhaps, the one we trust never trusted us. But did we ever stop to wonder why? How can they trust us? It is possible they do not trust themselves, so how could they trust another? But how could they betray you? It's possible they've been betrayed, and they don't know how to be a friend. Nevertheless, let's avoid this from happening again with a few steps:

1. Do not be so quick to call one a friend. Watch and pray! (Matt 26:41) That's what the Bible says.
2. Do not be so quick to judge one from their outward appearance. Get to know them and ask God to reveal their heart. The Bible says, **"A good man brings good things out of the good stored up in their heart, and an evil man brings evil**

things out of the evil stored up in his heart. **For the mouth speaks what the heart is full of.**" (Matthew 12: 34-35) After you watch and pray, talk to them, and listen! Do not ignore the red flags.

3. Believe what you see. If they mistreat their own brother and sister, trust me, they will mistreat you too!
4. Before calling one a friend, make sure you are everything you want them to be. This is just as important as the other three!

Journal Day 2

Let us look at who you are because we can't expect one to be a friend if we are not our own friend.

<u>Step 1:</u> Find a scripture to remind you of who you are to Christ.

<u>Step 2:</u> Be honest with yourself and write down all your attributes, including the good, bad, and ugly. (Take a few days to do a self-check and then write it down)

<u>Step 3</u>: After you discover "the real you" then you can make sure you surround yourself with people who enhance you and not ones who destroy you. Once you acknowledge the seat you are in, you will be able to place people in their rightful seat.

_____

_____

_____

_____

_____

_____

_____

DAY 3

TAKEN

"No, my brother! She cried. Don't be foolish! Don't do this to me!"
2 Samuel 13:12 NLT

She was only 19 years old, away from home for the first time in a land unfamiliar to her, but she wanted something different. A different life, a different scenario. You see, Chicago was not safe, all her friends were dying and the ones that were alive were not truly living. Having babies was the thing to do, but no one had a dream. No one talked about leaving Chicago, so she did. Moving across the map was always her dream. She wanted a fresh life, a life without struggle, a life without abuse, a life without lies, a whole new life! Those were dreams and she was going to do everything in her power to make them her reality until one day something was taken from her.

Knock, knock.
"Please come back," she yelled from the bathroom.
The knocking continued.

Naked as the day she came into this world, she grabbed a towel to dry off and as she walked out the bathroom, her room door opened. Her heart was racing, and water was dripping from her feet as she raced to stop whoever was trying to enter. Vulnerable, to say the least, but she was determined to do everything she could to stop that person on the other side of the door.

"WHO ARE YOU?" she screamed as she began punching the hands that were pushing the door.

It was nobody but God because she should have slipped from the water, but something in her told her to fight. In her mind, she had to survive. As she fought for what seemed like her life, she couldn't stop the endless questions that were flowing through her mind. *Who unlocked the door? How did we get to this place? Why me? And why in the world are they trying so hard to take something from her?*

In the Bible, when women were raped, retaliation took place. People were killed which meant that blood was on multiple hands. They did not leave room for God to handle the problem.

Journal Day 3

Who took something from you? What did they take?

Prepare to go to war right now! Make sure you are in a safe place and get your war cry ready. Prepare for the victory! (I like to play "War" by Pastor Charles Jenkins.)

Step 1: Write their names down.
Step 2: I challenge you to pray for them. Call their names out! Ask God to make them whole. I have learned that people take from others because they feel they are lacking something. So, pray for wholeness in their life.
Step 3: Pray against the spirit of rejection and the spirit of abandonment. Hurt people hurt people. (It's not right but it happens.)
Step 4: Ask God for forgiveness for harboring bitterness and resentment. You may not want to admit it but deep down you know this still hurts you and because you are hurting, you may have hurt

or offended someone that didn't do anything wrong to you. So repent!

Step 5: Identify what was taken. Was it your self-worth? Was it your smile? Was it your joy? Take some time and identify what was taken.

Step 6: Play your war song and let's take it back! Remember, the enemy comes to steal, kill, and destroy and we cannot give him anything that doesn't belong to him in the first place. So, let's take it back. Pray that God restores your peace, your joy, your smile and whatever else you gave him. Decree and declare, like David, that you will recover all! (1 Samuel 30:18)

_____

_____

_____

_____

_____

_____

_____

_____

_____

_____

_____

_____

_____

_____

_____

_____

DAY 4
CATCH AND RELEASE

"Now, the Lord provided a huge fish to swallow Jonah, and Jonah was in the belly of the fish three days and three nights. And the Lord commanded the fish, and it vomited Jonah onto dry land." Jonah 1:17, 2:10 NIV

She knew she had a calling on her life, but her flesh wanted what the world was offering. She wanted a relationship. She wanted to be loved but for some reason it seemed like the dating game was a game of "catch and release." You see, catch and release is a fisherman sport. They use a fishing pole and rod, but the hook is made differently from the one that other fishermen use who plan to catch a fish and eat it. The catch and release fishermen do everything other fishermen do except they throw the fish back. That was what she experienced in dating and maybe you feel the same way. It's like the men you meet do everything they are supposed to do or pretend they really want you when the reality is that dating is just a sport for them. They just want to see if they can catch you and when they do, they simply toss you back out there. Then you are left with a scar from the hook, awaiting to be captured again. JESUS!

In the book of Jonah, God had Jonah swallowed by a whale. After three days and three nights of prayer, God allowed the fish to vomit him up! I'm telling you that if you just pray before you become the prey, God will put you in a pond of fishermen that have been waiting all winter long to catch the biggest and best fish. They are eager to show their catch off to the world!

Your time is around the corner, but please begin to pray now. In His time, God will vomit you out of the wrong situation you are in so that you can go where He wants you to go and do whatever it is that He called you to do. So, what are you waiting for? Let's pray!

Journal Day 4

What relationship swallowed you up? What relationship set you back?

Step 1: Write their names down.
Step 2: For the next three days, Ask God to break any and every soul tie and pray for healing because some of them may still have a hook in you.
Step 3: Release them! Releasing them is not for them but it is allowing you to make room for the one that is meant for you.
Step 4: Stop procrastinating! Let them go!

_____

_____

_____

_____

_____

_____

_____

_____

_____

_____

_____

_____

DAY 5
SONSBAND

"A wise woman builds her home, but a foolish woman tears it down with her own hands." Proverbs 14:1 NLT

It finally happened! She found the man of her dreams. He is so supportive and loving; she could not wait to meet the woman who raised him. She wanted to tell her, "You raised a great man. Thank you." But to her surprise, his mother was not happy for him. She did not want him to grow up. She treated him like a child, and she talked to her future daughter-in-law as if she were a child as well. Why is this happening? She thought that mothers were supposed to raise their boys to be mighty and strong, strong, and courageous and independent!

She thought independence was the goal so that they could have all the tools to take care of their own families. But not his mother! This mother seemed as if she raised her son to be her *sonsband* -- her son and husband! Ugh! Disgusting! His mom wanted him to take care of her; she wanted to control his life.

She asked on more than one occasion, *"Lord, why is this happening? Who told her she was supposed to hinder his walk? And why does she think she has permission to talk to me as if I am some bum on the street?"* What a nightmare!

The Bible says a man is supposed to leave his household, his mother and father and cleave to his wife. (Genesis 2:24) What many fail to realize is that when a woman walks down the aisle it resembles the steps that she has taken to get to that point of marriage, and when she reaches her husband, the father releases her to be protected by the new man that will soon lead the household. The woman goes from one covering to another. Essentially, the father of the bride is saying, "I trust that you will take care of my daughter."

Therefore, mother of the groom, accept the process and welcome your new addition to the family. And remember what the Bible says, **"A wise woman builds her house, but a foolish one will tear it down with her own hands."** Today, choose to be wise.

Journal Day 5

Have you experienced this before? Are you the bride or groom? Or are you even considering marrying into this situation?

Steps for Bride or Groom

Step 1: Pray before you enter this covenant. The Bible says that the Lord will perfect everything which concerns you! (Psalm 138:8) So, write it down.
Step 2: Do not rush into the covenant, wait until the smoke clears.
Step 3: Invite the mother for a heart to heart conversation.

Steps for Wife and Husband

Step 1: Write the mother-in-law's name down.
Step 2: Pray and ask the Lord to grant you a heart of flesh so you can forgive her because she knows not what she does. (Ezekiel 36:26)
Step 3: Pray that she gains wisdom to do the right thing.

DAY 6
THE STING

"They surrounded me like bees."
Psalm 118:12

"A BEE!" She screamed as she heard the buzzing. Scared as she could be, she kept running. Even though she did not actually see it, she heard it loud and clear and that was enough to keep her running. Unaware if the bee was still chasing her, out of breath and all, she kept running because the thought of being stung by a bee was less than desirable. Oh, how she wished she could hear the buzzing of the enemy before the sting. You better believe she would have run away!

It was the best summer of her life: new job, new car, new look, just a NEW LIFE! She was ahead of the game: young, single, saved with no kids. Then one day she was approached by this fine man. Did you hear me? That brother was FINE! Only if she knew then what she knows now, she would have run. He was charming, very educated, wealthy, single, no kids and nothing to hide--or so she thought. After months of spending time with him, different women began popping up, some from out of town and some local. It was a mess!

There was no way she could stay in that relationship, when truly she was the only one committed. She could not take it! The thought of being faithful to someone that was not faithful to her tore her insides up. Then the buzzing began.

"You stupid!"
"Girl, I'm going to hook him up with my friend."

"If I were single, I would take him off the market."

"I knew she would mess this up."

"REALLY?! SHUT UP," she wanted to scream but her heart was broken into so many pieces that she did not have the energy to fight back. If only after the sting, the enemy dies, like a real bee, she could have still been standing.

Two things occur when a bee stings its prey:

#1: The bee's stinger gets lodged into its prey and the bee cannot remove it because it is made of two barbed lancets. Therefore, a bee stings with the intention to hurt, but not only does it leave the stinger, but it also leaves part of its digestive tract plus muscles and nerves. This ultimately kills the bee.

#2: The bee releases pheromones that stir up nearby bees, which can lead to multiple attacks! It only takes one bee to attack. That bee then signals other bees to finish the job.

That is exactly what killed her spirit. She went from being an independent woman to a broken woman in a matter of months. The spirit of embarrassment almost took her out, but God! She made promises to herself to make sure that did not happen to her again.

Promise #1: Stay far away from those bees.

Promise #2: Above all else, guard your heart! (Proverbs 4:23)

Promise #3: Create a friendship first, then build from there.

Journal Day 6

Let's talk about these bees! Do you find yourself committing to someone who does not commit to you? Have you ever dealt with the spirit of embarrassment?

Step 1: Write down what happened.

Step 2: Fellowship first! Learn to be cordial. Remember, you must guard your heart! You can be cordial without becoming friends. This will eliminate one becoming a frienemy!

Step 3: Pray and ask God to show you the heart of the people around you. The word says man looks at the outward and the Lord looks at the heart. (1 Samuel 16:7) Ask God to reveal their heart and believe what you see!

_____

_____

_____

_____

_____

_____

_____

_____

_____

_____

_____

_____

_____

_____

_____

_____

_____

_____

DAY 7
REVENGE

"Do not take revenge, my dear friends, but leave room for God's wrath, for it is written: "It is mine to avenge, I will repay," says the Lord."
Romans 12:19 NIV

Have you ever been caught in a crossfire? Have you ever felt like, "I did nothing for them to treat me this way"? Envy is a cruel and vicious disease that kills one soul and if not careful, can seep to everyone around you. When this happens, the only thing left to do is take REVENGE! Or should you?

She was ridiculed and put to shame in front of the entire staff. Their goal was to dim the light, and not only did they want to dim the light, but they wanted to blow it out completely. But she wouldn't have it! Even though they lied about her, defamed her character, talked about her child, and yet smiled in her face when she walked inside the room, she didn't stop being herself. But then it happened! The insidious behavior rubbed off on the manager and what seemed to be tolerable became unbearable and REVENGE was on the forefront of her mind.

She couldn't believe it. The manager began to humiliate her in front of the staff and that's when her light began to dim. She had never experienced that before and even though she was discouraged, something in her wouldn't allow her to become the thing she hated. Therefore, she did what she was taught to do...PRAY!

While in prayer, she would hear, "Be angry but sin not." That should have been enough, but it wasn't until this quote came across her eyes that she began to see things differently. The quote by

Confucius stated, "Before you embark on a journey of revenge, first dig 2 graves." *Ouch!!* That hit her differently. The thoughts started running through her mind. *"Do I want to make a grave for myself or should I just allow them to bury themselves?"* She went back into prayer and the Lord spoke.

First she heard, "My child, they lied on Jesus, so please don't think they won't lie on you!" Then she heard, "Do not take revenge, my dear friends, but leave room for God's wrath, for it is written: It is mine to avenge: I will repay," says the Lord.

That encouraged her and a flood of scriptures began to flow through her: "NO WEAPON FORMED AGAINST YOU SHALL PROSPER, AND EVERY TONGUE WHICH RISES AGAINST YOU IN JUDGEMENT YOU SHALL CONDEMNED! (Isaiah 54:17) Oh wow, she thought as she cried out! And with great humility she accepted the calling on her life and with confidence, she knew then the Lord would fight for her!

The question is, Do you believe the Lord will fight for you?

Journal Day 7

Have you been ridiculed or put to shame? Have you been lied on or even persecuted?

Step 1: Identify those who were out to shame you. I mean the ones you wanted to take revenge on.
Step 2. Present those names to the Father!
Step 3: Believe the word of the Lord! NO WEAPON THAT IS FORMED AGAINST YOU SHALL PROSPER and know with confidence that the Lord will vindicate you!

DAY 8

BLINDSPOT

"But who can discern their own errors? Forgive my hidden faults."
Psalm 19:12 NIV

A blind spot in a vehicle is an area around the vehicle that cannot be directly observed by the driver. To see those blind spots, the driver must adjust his or her position by checking over his or her shoulder. But what about a person in your spiritual blind spot? If that person is unaware that someone or something is in an area or around them because they cannot directly see them, an accident is sure to happen.

He thought he was in control of his own life. Not only was he married but he had a live-in girlfriend and because he was indulging in sin, he was spiritually blind. You could not tell him he was wrong and that he was driving on the opposite side of the road because he surrounded himself with others who were riding with him and would not correct him. So, to hear, "you're going the wrong way" was confusing to him because his family and "friends" cheered him on as he led the way.

His *real* friends recognized what a disaster he was living because his "girlfriend" had that "bag" and helped with the upkeep of his wife's house. Yet, he would not listen to his friends. Living a lie and living in sin was going to be the death of him. With a broken heart and a broken mirror, he could not see the blind spot. And because his new crowd did not look over their own shoulders, they did not have the ability to look over his either.

BOOM! BAM!

The crash occurred and all he was left with was his blues to unfold.

"Lord, help me," he cried out and God showed him his hidden faults. God took him and placed him in the right lane and gave him a second chance to get things right. Our prayers are that he stays the course and that you do too!

Journal Day 8

What or who is in your blind spot? (You may not know because it is an area you cannot see)

Step 1: Have a talk with your real friends about what they see that you may not see.
Step 2: Pray and ask God to reveal the truth about what your friends told you.
Step 3: Make the necessary adjustments and proceed to live upright.

_____

_____

_____

_____

_____

_____

_____

_____

_____

_____

_____

DAY 9
STD

"On hearing this, Jesus said, "It is not the healthy who need a doctor, but the sick." Matthew 9:12 NIV

Sexually Transmitted Disease (STD) is common in the world. As a matter of fact, according to the CDC, Center of Disease Control, there are an estimated 20 million new infections that occur every year in the United States. Wow, that is some food for thought but fortunately, that is not the disease this brother faced. The brother faced a Spiritually Transmitted Disease, STD, and he encountered it the same way, through a sexual contact caused by bacteria, viruses and or a parasite.

This brother was new to the city; he left home in hopes to start a new life. He joined a church and in months he was back into the same mess he tried to run away from. You see, he carried the STD, he was the parasite, and unknowingly, he connected to another host. If we knew the numbers, I am sure CDC would estimate 50 million infections every year. See, the difference between the sexually transmitted and the spiritually transmitted disease is that a medical doctor cannot diagnose the spiritual disease and give you something to take for a few days to clear your system. No, it's not that easy.

A person with a spiritually transmitted disease can carry the disease and infect others and the disease can continue to spread until the curse is broken. The only way to break the chain is by prayer and fasting, but first someone must recognize they are carrying the disease. The symptoms are not burning and itching in your genitals but burning and itching in the flesh. Symptoms are fornication, hatred, sexual immorality, pornography, witchcraft, alcoholism, substance abuse, fear, cursing and negative thinking. If you allow these things to continue, they become a stronghold in your life and ultimately, you become a walking spiritual disease, transmitting it to everyone you encounter.

Nonetheless, you have access to the best doctor around! Jesus said, "It's not the healthy that needs help, it's the sick!"

Journal Day 9

Are you sick?

Step 1: Identify the spiritual diseases you are carrying.

Step 2: Identify the spiritual diseases you have transmitted.

Step 3: Take a few days and pray about them both and cast down every stronghold! (2 Corinthians 10:4)

_____

_____

_____

_____

_____

_____

_____

_____

_____

_____

DAY 10
GET OUT!

"Get out your country, from your family and from your father's house..."
Genesis 12:1 NKJV

Can you imagine the thoughts flowing through Abraham's mind when God told him to *get out? But where am I supposed to go? I must leave the country, leave my family, and get out my father's house and THEN WHAT?* How many can be honest and say that once we heard the words 'get out,' everything after would have been a blur.

It was five days before Christmas of 2015 when his family put him out. See, he already knew it was time to go, but sometimes we can get comfortable in the resting place when that is not the destination. He quickly learned that God will put you in an uncomfortable position and sometimes He will put you out of a place just so that you can complete what He started in you! This young man was put out of his family's home, a comfortable place, and he had nowhere to go. So, the journey began.

This fella exhausted his bank account sleeping in different hotels, trying to get comfortable and once the money ran out, he began couch surfing. He stayed at different friends' houses, but he could not get comfortable. Then one day, exhausted from all the moving around, he stopped and cried out to the Lord and said, "I have nothing. I have no place to go and I have no money to eat. I have been living out of my car which I cannot pay the car note nor the insurance. I can barely put gas in this thing. Are you going to take that as well?"

Then a small whisper said, "Get from under thy kindreds house..." He heard it over the next few days so he decided to search the words in his phone and a Bible scripture appeared and it said, ***"Get thee out of thy country, and from thy kindred, and from thy father's house, unto a land that I will shew you." (Genesis 12:1 KJV)*** Oh, how he was confused, but he didn't give up. Instead he searched for another version to help clarify what God was speaking to him.

The Lord had said to Abram, "Go from your country, your people and your father's household to the land I will show you. I will make you into a great nation, and I will bless you. I will make your name great, and you will be a blessing. I will bless those who bless you, and whoever curses you I will curse, and all peoples on earth will be blessed through you.

According to Google, in 2019, there were about 567,715 homeless people in the United States of America. Can you imagine their stories? If your family put you out, ask God to show you the land He has for you. You never know, that may be where your blessing is! So, stop procrastinating. Get out and find your land!

Journal Day 10

Are you settling? Are you in a resting place? Or have you been put out?

Step 1: Be honest with yourself. Where have you stayed too long?
Step 2: Do you believe God has something great in store for you?
Step 3: Pray and ask God where you should go or what you should do.

_____

_____

_____

_____

DAY 11
SUFFOCATING

"Then Saul dressed David in his own tunic."
1 Samuel 17:38

The story of David and Goliath is a very memorable story, but I can't help but think of Saul and David's relationship. It started with Saul trying to dress David in his armor. While reading this passage, I always stop and think, "Why would one expect another to dress like him, look like him, or smell like him?" That will never work because they are two different people. I imagine interviewing David and hearing him say, "That relationship with Saul was spiritually suffocating."

Spiritual suffocation can happen when one is trying to control your walk with Christ. The hindrance is so heavy that you feel entangled with the way they view God when before you met them, you could hear God clearly. Now, you are spiritually suffocating because they have used their natural power to overpower the voice of God.

He thought he found the right mentor. He felt like Ruth when she told Naomi, **"Your people will be my people and your God my God. (Ruth 1:16)** But suddenly things changed. At first, they were studying the word of God together. The oil on their lives complemented each other until the congregation began to lean toward the mentee and not the mentor. This made the mentor MAD! Frustrated and confused, the mentor began to mistreat the mentee in public. He began criticizing him on live television, saying things like, "What do you have on?" and "Camera man, please zoom in on these shoes." He plainly tore him down just so that he could remind the mentee who was in charge while laughing at him. Some days the mentee would cry out loud and other days he would cry in silence. The embarrassment that he took was shameful and especially when the mentor would embarrass him in front of his family.

One day, he decided to say the words of David. *"I cannot go with these." (1 Samuel 17:39)* The mentee decided to go back to the place he always hears from God and cried out. What the mentee didn't expect was for the people to pray with him; he was not alone. The people saw what the mentor was doing, and they encouraged the mentee to be strong. And just like David, he got rid of everything that tried to choke the life out of him; he got rid of the garments, moved out the house, avoided unnecessary encounters, and hid. This might sound crazy, but if David can do it so can you!

Journal Day 11

Do you feel like you are being suffocated (trapped and oppressed)?

Step 1: Identify what or who is causing the suffocation. Write it down.
Step 2: Understand that your life is important and remember what the word of God says concerning you! "For I know the plans I have for you" declares the Lord, "plans to prosper you and not to harm you, plans to give you hope and a future." (Jeremiah 29:11)
Step 3: Pray and ask God to open a new door but understand this could be ordained. Therefore, "Seek first the kingdom of God, and his righteousness; and all these things shall be added unto you." (Matthew 6:33)

DAY 12

HIDDEN SCAR

"But he was pierced for our transgression, he was crushed for our iniquities; the punishment that brought us peace was upon him, and by his wounds we are healed." Isaiah 53:5 NIV

It was love at first sight. He couldn't believe what was right in front of him, yet he was crushed because he couldn't have what was presented to him. For the first time in his life, his heart was bleeding because he found true love, but he couldn't take her as his wife because his ex-girlfriend was pregnant. Therefore, she got the ring and his rights.

Thirty years passed as he pretended to love his wife, but his heart was still with his true love. He knew he broke her heart, but he couldn't fathom not being a part of his kids' lives. Yet empty inside and full of regret, he continued his routine. Go to work, take care of the family, and make sure the kids experienced a two-parent household. He told himself that he couldn't run from his responsibilities, but he also didn't want to run from the love that pierced his heart. And though he battled for years, he made sure to hide that part of his heart to make sure he smiled for the kids.

Aching inside, he did not know when or if it was ever going to happen. He also didn't know that his wife knew that his heart was with another. She heard his late-night cries, and she knew at times he was depressed. However, she too thought about the kids and she stayed for the same reasons he did.

Well, enough was enough! The kids were grown, and he couldn't take it anymore. What was hidden was exposed. He got the divorce, and he went looking for the woman he hadn't seen in thirty years.

And guess what? He found her! To his disbelief, she never stopped thinking about him either. She stated that she tried to hide the love inside, but everyone knew that her heart was with him. She too had lived with the hidden scar.

She asked him, "How did you hold on?" He replied, "I never loved anyone like this. I tried to move on, but I couldn't." Then he asked her the same question, but her reply was different. She said, "I honestly couldn't bear the pain; therefore, I began to read the Bible and to my surprise, I learned that there was one who endured much more pain than me. I knew if he could heal then so could I." She continued to tell him that she felt betrayed but God's words healed her. She quoted, **"But he was pierced for our transgression, he was crushed for our iniquities; the punishment that brought us peace was upon him, and by his wounds we are healed."** She made sure to tell him how that scripture got her through the years and every time she read it, her heart was filled with forgiveness and it still beat for him. Not wasting any more time, they married immediately and haven't looked back. And guess what, the kids are happy for them as well!

Journal Day 12

What's your hidden scar? We all have them, whether it's seen or unseen. Nonetheless, by His stripes, you are healed!

Step 1: Identify your hidden scar. (Is it grief, hurt, bad memories, betrayal from a loved one or a surgery that no one knows about? What is it?)

Step 2: Remind yourself that healing is the children's bread. (Matthew 15:26 KJV)

Step 3: Fast with this prayer. Fasting demonstrates the depth of your desire when praying for something. (The number of days to fast is between you and God.)

DAY 13

STICKS AND STONES

"Gentle words bring life and health; a deceitful tongue crushes the spirit."
Proverbs 15:4 NLT

Whoever said sticks and stones may break your bones, but words will never hurt you, lied! The word of God says that the power of life and death is in the tongue. Therefore, if you are speaking death, those words hurt! But God! He will curse those who curse you and bless those who bless you.

She once met this very rude woman who was an identical twin. When she met her sister, she could tell them apart right away because the twin was much thinner. She asked the rude twin had she been bigger than her sister her entire life. She was just curious how that may have made her feel. The woman shared how their father favored her sister more because she was thinner. With confusion, she asked, "How did you come up with that?" The woman responded, "Because they would say things like, 'Oh, your sister is prettier,' or 'She is much thinner.'" The young woman was always instructed to lose some weight. She could see the pain in her eyes when the woman shared her story and she sympathized with her. She also understood why the woman was so rude and why she thought it was ok to tear people down with her words. The rude twin was only doing to others what was done to her.

Why do we feel we have to break each other down with name calling? Is this a way to make ourselves feel better? Do you feel better when you know your words have affected another? Or could it be that someone verbally abused you and you know exactly how it feels? Therefore, instead of rewriting the wrong, you continue crushing someone else's spirit with your words. Well, do yourself and the world a favor. Write these words down and memorize them: *Gentle words bring life and health, but a deceitful tongue crushes the spirit.* Today, I pray you choose to speak life.

Journal Day 13

Understand that stick and stones break bones and words break spirits. Has your spirit been crushed by words?

Step 1: Let's rewrite some wrongs. Write down some phrases that people said to you that hurt you.

Step 2: Draw a line through those phrases and underneath, write some encouraging words you would rather hear.

Step 3: Repeat those encouraging words to yourself. If no one else will encourage you, you sure can! Remember, David encouraged himself in the Lord. (1 Samuel 30:6)

_____

_____

_____

_____

_____

_____

_____

_____

_____

_____

DAY 14
I CAN'T BREATHE

"This is what the sovereign Lord says: Look! I am going to put breath into you and make you live again!" Ezekiel 37:5 NLT

The police are not the enemy; however, neither should the color of your skin be. Being Black in the United States is not the most popular thing. In 2019, 164 Black men and women were killed by the police. Why? Is being black a crime? Or is there a new law that says, "Kill every black person you see?"

This season reminds me of the story of Moses, where the Pharaoh of Egypt decreed that all Hebrew baby boys had to be drowned at birth because he feared they would be too powerful (Exodus 1:22). But Moses' mom hid him. (Exodus 2:3) You see, just like Moses, there is a calling on your life and even though it doesn't seem like it, everyone knows it! Why do you think the enemy is trying to muzzle you? It's because he sees the greatness in you. The problem is that you don't see the greatness in yourself, but don't worry God will hide you too! His word says, *"He who dwells in the secret place of the most High shall abide under the shadow of the Almighty."* (Psalm 91:1)

I know that this passage won't bring any of the 164 strong lives back, neither will it bring back any of the Hebrew babies, but I want to remind you that your life matters and you are valuable! If the *sovereign Lord says, Look! I am going to put breath into you and make you live again,* then you shall live again! Don't allow the media or anyone to put fear in you because if God is for you, He is more than the world against you. (Romans 8:31) The enemy knows that you were made in God's image and our likeness (Genesis 1:26) and that's the very reason he is afraid of you. So, do yourself a favor. Breathe and live again!

Journal Day 14

Do you understand that we wrestle not against flesh and blood? (Ephesians 6:12)

Step 1: Write and express your feelings about this devotional. Did you lose anyone to police brutality? How does the Black Lives Matter movement affect you?

Step 2: Make an intentional effort to give everything that you are feeling to God. The Bible says to cast all your cares unto Him. (1 Peter 5:7)

Step 3: Pray and ask God to change things! I am praying for change, how about you?

_____

_____

_____

_____

_____

_____

_____

_____

_____

_____

_____

DAY 15
MISCARRIAGE

"Oh, God-of-the-Angel-Armies, If you'll take a good, hard look at my pain..." 1 Samuel 1:9-11 The Message

Singing, "Girl and boy sitting in the tree, K-I-S-S-I-N-G! First comes love. Then comes marriage. Then comes baby in the baby carriage." Oh, how I remember the good ole days when we sat around and sang that song when we thought we were in love with the first boy we kissed. Ha! What that song did not teach us was that boy and girl would fall in love and instead of the baby in the carriage, girl and boy could possibly experience a miscarriage.

It was three months into their blissful marriage when suddenly, the pain in her abdominal area began to cramp like no other. The pain was unbearable, but she was unaware of the pain that would follow the news she would soon get. She carried on with her day because she thought it was just a horrible menstrual, but then the bleeding began, and the cramping intensified. However, she continued with business as usual because being a woman is not easy and she was used to enduring pain. But something in her told her that time was different.

She called her doctor to schedule a checkup because the bleeding was heavy, the cramps were unbearable, and she hadn't done anything differently. She just needed to be on the safe side. A day before the appointment, she had the urge to have a bowel movement, but she passed several large blood clots instead. When she called her doctor, she was instructed to come in as soon as possible. Labs were drawn and the anticipation was horrid, but finally another lab and then the news came. "I'm sorry to tell you but your body rejected the baby."

Wait, I was pregnant? Why would my body reject the baby? Isn't that what we are made for?

Devastation hit like never before! The next few days were not blissful but a blur. At that point it had to be a bad dream and she just wanted to be awakened. The abdominal pain was nothing compared to the pain in her heart. She did not want to hear that everything would be okay because to her it was not. She did not want to hear that she would get through it because at that point she did not see how! But God is a very present help in a time of trouble (Psalm 46:1).

She began to worship and cry out to God and she fell into a deep sleep. When she awakened, she felt some relief but then God spoke through a Pastor on TV. He was preaching about Hannah. She heard something and she held onto it. *"Before the year is out, Hannah had conceived and given birth to a son."* (1 Samuel 1:20 MSG) The pastor said to remove Hannah's name and place your name. For the next several weeks, she did just that. And a year later, she conceived and gave birth to a son.

Journal Day 15

Have you experienced a miscarriage? Or are you barren? I must be honest and say, THIS IS A FAITH WALK!

Step 1: You must hear from God and God Alone! Do not allow the doctor's report to be your end all.

Step 2: You must present facts along with faith to God on this one. (example: You did it for Hannah and you did it for Sarah. (Genesis 21:1) Surely, you can do it for me, God!)

Step 3: Don't doubt just believe the report from the Lord!

DAY 16

INFATUATION ABUSE

"Create in me a clean heart, O God: and renew a right spirit within me."
Psalm 51:10 KJV

She hurt so many men and honestly, she did not care how she left them to feel. She was worse than men who perfected the catch and release. She had an addiction, an intense but short-lived passion or admiration for someone, but she abused every man she met. You know, like substance abuse or alcohol abuse. Her abuse was infatuation. She loved the intense feeling that she got in the beginning of a relationship and when that was over, she was done. On to the next!

She thought the dating game was over for her. In her eyes, she finally met the man of her dreams. She devoted herself to him. Like Ruth, she laid at his feet and not at his side because she wanted him to respect her and she did not want to displease him. (Ruth 3:4) Sex was out of the question! But her old behavior caught up with her. You see, it is this thing called sowing and reaping that she didn't know about until she submitted to Christ and that thing came and bit a sister right back. She wanted to spend the rest of her life with him; turns out he didn't feel the same.

Months later, she was diagnosed with a broken heart and while in the hospital crying out, she knew that she was reaping what she had sown all those years. Right then and there she prayed, "Create in me a clean heart and renew the right spirit within me." She asked God to forgive her of her past sin and to give her another chance and He did! God allowed her to feel what she made others feel. But that day she promised to put God first, to love what/who He loves, and to make sure she prays about every man entering her life. She understood that the heart was fragile, and she had to guard not only her heart but the heart of those she met. (Proverbs 4:23) This lesson profoundly changed her life.

Journal Day 16

Have you experienced a broken heart? Have you experienced or are you going through something that can change your life?

Step 1: Be honest with yourself. Do you battle with infatuation abuse?
Step 2: Assess your past relationships. Have you felt that you only attract those who have the addiction?
Step 3: Pray and ask God to renew the right spirit within you. Sometimes we attract what is in us. Therefore, make a change so you can attract something new!

_____

_____

_____

_____

_____

_____

_____

_____

_____

_____

_____

DAY 17
THE ASSIGNMENT

"When the Lord began to speak through Hosea, the Lord said to him, "Go marry a promiscuous woman and have children with her, for like an adulterous wife this land is guilty of unfaithfulness to the Lord." Hosea 1:2

Do you think it is necessary for God to pair up a godly man with an ungodly woman? Is it possible for you to say you love a God that you do not see but hate a brother or sister that you see?

God wants us to love the world as He loves and that is why He paired Hosea with Gomer, who was the exact opposite. *"For God so loved the world, that he gave his only begotten son." (John 3:16)* The passage doesn't say, "For God so loved the godly that He gave..." No! It says, "For God so loved the **world**..." and to truly express how much He loved the world, He placed emphasis by saying, "**so** loved." So, why are we so quick to judge the Gomers (ungodly). Have you ever wondered how they feel about being the adulterer? Or if they were sad because they felt unworthy to repent?

In a world full of sin and deceit, we can never face our own truth, especially if we are surrounded by worldly people. That is why God has given us the assignment to connect and with those who don't know Him yet. No matter how embarrassing it may be, or how tiring it may be to love someone that does not love you the same, or how unequal it seems, God did not make a mistake when He paired you with the total opposite. He wants you to put yourself in their shoes. He wants you to experience true humility. This is your assignment! This process will sharpen you, mature you and have you to experience agape love. So, do not give up on them because God didn't give up on you!

Journal Day 17

Is your spouse your assignment or did you choose the wrong person?

Step 1: Be honest with your reality? Is this what you imagined or dreamed?
Step 2: Express to God how this relationship makes you feel.
Step 3: Get help and seek counseling! Just remember, God is the Wonderful Counselor! (Isaiah 9:6)

_____

_____

_____

_____

_____

_____

_____

_____

_____

_____

_____

_____

_____

_____

_____

_____

DAY 18

COMPARISON KILLS

"When his brothers saw that their father loved him more than any of them, they hated him all the more." Genesis 37:4-5 NIV

Could you imagine being born into a large family, being the youngest and your brothers being jealous of you? Life is already hard as it is, your co-workers are jealous, your classmates are jealous and even your family members! Wow! Why can't we all just get along?

I can only imagine how Joseph felt with his brothers hating him *all the more*. This passage is hard to read, let alone break it down because hate is a strong word. It literally means a very intense or passionate dislike for someone. My question is how do you allow yourself to get to that point where you hate someone? Like Cain, he was so jealous of his brother that he killed him. (Genesis 4:8) To me, there is nothing my brothers could do or say that would make me hate them. However, if you are comparing yourself to others, that can stir some things up. Comparison kills, it steals, and it destroys. Comparison tells everyone that you are not happy with yourself. (You can change your circumstances, but the question is are you willing?)

All the time you are taking to tear another person down, you could have been using that energy to build yourself up. The next time your mind wonders and tells you to investigate another person's background, do yourself a favor and research your next school, or the city you may want to reside in, or even your next career move. Do not allow comparison to steal your joy because I have learned that every fiery dart that you throw at others, seven more may come back in your direction. Plus, God is always watching. Joseph's brothers thought they were getting away with selling him, but Joseph's dreams came true; he ruled over them! (Genesis 41:41-44) They ended up needing him and at first, he was punishing them, but he forgave them. Cain was also punished by God. He had to live with a curse given to him by God.(Genesis 4:11) So, make sure you reroute your attention and your anger because nothing compares to the wrath of God!

Journal Day 18

Understand that comparing yourself will not fix your present situation.

Step 1: Stop comparing yourself. Period!
Step 2: Write down some things you would like to accomplish, create a plan to make them happen, and do it!
Step 3: If you are having a hard time with this, ask a successful friend to help guide you in the right direction.

_____

_____

_____

_____

_____

_____

_____

_____

_____

DAY 19

THE PIT EXPERIENCE

"And they took him and cast him into the pit. The pit was empty; there was no water in it." Genesis 37:24 KJV

If you have read the book of Genesis, this story of Joseph could tear you apart. First, they hated him *all the more*, then they compared themselves, but it didn't stop there. The hatred intensified to a level where they decided to kill their own flesh and blood. He was just a kid and together they took him and threw him in an empty pit. Therefore, if he did not die from the fall then he would die from thirst! But God! What was intended for evil will always turn out for your good. (Genesis 50:20) However, just like Joseph, no one knows the end of their personal story so all you can do is weep while you are hoping and praying that the fall won't take you out.

It was 2015 when he was fighting for his life. His family hated him *all the more*. They made up stories about him, attacked him verbally, and then put him out. Not to mention the job that he had just started. They counteracted his salary and decreased his wages. He could not believe all that was happening but just when he thought it could not get any worse, he broke his foot. *"Wow,"* he thought. *"This cannot be happening to me."* He always knew the devil could not hit a moving target, but this catastrophe left him in a pit, "a dark place." He was empty and alone with no one to turn to because it was his family that had turned on him which led him to that place. He began to battle with depression and darkness became his friend. Day in and day out, he welcomed the darkness. His friends did not know what to do or how to help.

Nonetheless, God is the same God, yesterday, today, and forever. (Hebrews 13:8) Just as he pulled Joseph out the pit, he did the same for that man. It wasn't perfect at first, but every day it got a little brighter. I want you to know that you may be having a pit experience, but God will show up for you like He always does. Just do yourself a favor and welcome the Light!

Journal Day 19

Have you ever been in a pit environment? Do you experience sibling rivalry or hatred from your co-workers or classmates?

Step 1: What happened? Write it down!
Step 2: Re-evaluate yourself and be mindful who you share your dreams with.
Step 3: Share your dreams with God. He will make sure you reach them.
Step 4: Forgive those who tried to set you up!

_____

_____

_____

_____

_____

_____

_____

_____

DAY 20
COVID-19

"Yea, though I walk through the valley of the shadow of death, I will fear no evil, For You are with me." Psalm 23:4 NKJV

In 2003, a group of Marines reported to the base. About 10,000 reservists were recalled to fight the war on terrorism. What was unexpected was for five women to be in her room when she got there. She sat and talked to them; one was planning a wedding, and another had just given birth, but none of them wanted to go to Afghanistan. What is memorable about that night is that she had an attitude about them being in her room when those ladies had no idea if they were ever going to return home. Nightmares still chase her as she was the one preparing their memorial services. Not sure what exactly happened but with the 1,000 or so memorial services they prepared for, she remembered most were killed by an IED, Improvised Explosive Devices. They were briefed on the devices and told that they were hidden, buried on the roads but during a convoy they needed to prepare for the unexpected.

Having to relive those moments have brought more sleepless nights as the reports continue to roll in. Now, she is faced with another unforeseen weapon called COVID-19. This time around, the veterans who survived Vietnam are being killed by this novel virus and those that survived Operation Freedom are now being forced to expect the unexpected in the "Land of the Free." However, we are at war again with an unforeseen, unknown virus that has killed over 200,000 people and infected millions.

With a racing heart and sweaty palms, she stands by as a procession passes as another soldier has died due to COVID-19. What a year 2020 has been and as she prays she can hear the scripture in her ear, "Yea, though I walk through the valley of the shadow of death, I will fear no evil; for thou art with me; thy rod and thy staff they comfort me." No matter what you have faced during this season, I want to remind you to be kind to people because you never know when their hour will come. Jesus said, *"In this world you may have trouble. But take heart! I have overcome this world."* (John 16:33b) Amen.

Journal Day 20

How have you handled the lockdown and everything that came with COVID-19? Did you lose anyone to COVID-19? What did you learn about yourself that you were able to change?

Step 1: Write it down. Remember to cast your cares to the Lord. (1 Peter 5:7)
Step 2: Be honest about how you feel. The Lord is close to the brokenhearted. (Psalm 34:18)
Step 3: Find the blessing in this storm. (Example: Were you able to spend more time with your family? Were you able to get the rest your body needed? Or did you reconnect with a loved one or relative?)

DAY 21

SHACKLES

"About midnight Paul and Silas were praying and singing hymn to God, and the other prisoners were listening to them. Suddenly there was such a violent earthquake that the foundations of the prison were shaken. At once all the prison doors flew open and everyone's chains came loose."
Acts 16:25-26 NIV

When growing up, we were always told when you do the wrong thing there will be consequences, but no one warned us that when you believe in Christ and you do the right thing, consequences would still come. Who is prepared for being punished for doing the right thing?

COVID came and not only did it bring about hundreds of thousands of deaths, but it also brought chaos and confusion, which led to division, which also caused an evil spirit to rise on the earth. I am not sure if I am clear, but the wrong was being rewarded and goodness was being frowned upon and ridiculed.

In June of 2020, a hospital team reunited after being divided since things were shut down. Due to COVID, half the team began working from home while the rest of the team had to go into the hospital; this caused an uproar! What the half of the team who worked from home did not expect was for the darkness in the room to rise and attack them. Out the blue, one spirit rose and started to yell, "IF YOU HAVEN'T BEEN HERE THAN YOU SHOULDN'T SAY ANYTHING." Everyone looked at the boss because surely, he was not going to allow this to happen. But to their surprise he turned his head, giving that demonic spirit permission to continue the attack and it did. When everyone noticed this spirit, the Light in the room put her hands up and asked, "Why all the hostility?" The evil spirit got out the chair and began to point her finger toward the Light yelling, "I'M NOT TALKING TO YOU, MIND YOUR OWN BUSINESS AND GO HOME! Again, the boss turned his head and said nothing.

"*What just happened*," thought the Light in the room? "*I sure hope they do not think they will get away with this.*" What occurred over the next few weeks was nothing but the devil. The evil spirits gathered to harass the Light, they lied on her, they laughed at her and they tried their best to destroy her. She felt that some spiritual shackles had been placed on her because she could not move without being attacked and after a while depression came knocking at her door. She could not sleep. But God! Just like Paul and Silas, she began to worship, and a violent earthquake shook the department, and a divine reversal took place! Glory Hallelujah! What the enemy tried to hold down was released! The Light felt those shackles fall off and a spirit of peace came through the department.

I am not sure if you feel bound down by the cares of this world, but I dare you to shout! I dare you to worship our King and I am sure your spiritual shackles shall fall.

Journal Day 21

You made it to the last day of this 21-day journey and this devotion was about being released and set free! Hallelujah!

<u>Step 1:</u> Write down everything that made you feel broken, destroyed, abused, and shattered!

<u>Step 2:</u> Tear this page out and rip it apart. It's time to destroy the things that tried to destroy you!

<u>Step 3:</u> Rejoice and rewrite your story!

<u>Step 4:</u> Take a blank sheet of paper and write what you would like to see and present that to God. *Write the vision and make it plain.* (Habakkuk 2:2)

_____

_____

_____

_____

_____

_____

_____

_____

_____

_____

_____

_____

_____

_____

PRAYER

Father, I thank You for the person holding this book! I pray that You show them your reckless love. I pray that YOU take them deeper than their feet could ever wander, and I pray that their faith will be made stronger. I pray that You allow them to forgive those who hurt them because, Lord, only You know how often they hurt You and You always forgive us.

Father, I pray YOU open doors that have been closed and I pray that You bless them indeed! Lord, enlarge their territory and give them strength to tell everyone about the grace and mercies that You have bestowed upon them.

Father, right now, I bind the spirit of depression, and oppression. Your word says, whatever we bind on earth will be bound in heaven and whatever you loose on earth will be loosed in heaven. Well, Father, I bind depression and I bind any suicidal thoughts right now in the name of Jesus. I pray for the comforter to place a blanket of peace over their minds and hearts. Lord, I come against the prince of the air, I bind him, and I command him to go back to the pits of hell from which he comes. And finally, I pray against any backlash, in Jesus' Name. I pray for sweet sleep and I pray for miracles, signs, and wonders.

Thank You, Lord, for your presence and we thank YOU for protecting us from dangers seen and unseen.

Lord, may you continue to watch over us and keep us in Jesus' name and I plead the blood of Jesus over this prayer, AMEN!

ABOUT THE AUTHOR

Shamika White is a depression survivor, a devoted wife, loving mother and faithful friend. She is a missionary who has traveled to Mexico, Dominican Republic and Honduras three times to provide care to the underserved. She is also a United States Navy veteran who served alongside the United States Marines in Camp Fuji, Japan; Camp Pendleton, California and Camp Lejeune, North Carolina.   While serving during Operation Enduring Freedom (OEF) and Operation Iraqi Freedom (OIF), Shamika served as a Chaplain's Assistant who provided combat stress support to active duty members and spouses.

Shamika is the founder of Blues' UnVeil, an organization aimed to promote awareness for individuals who suffer or have suffered from any form of depression. She is the founder of I.C.A.R.E. Collection, a collection of gifts geared to show one you care. Shamika received her Bachelor's of Science degree from University of St. Francis in Joliet, IL. in healthcare leadership with a concentration in training and development.

Currently, Shamika is serving veterans with PTSD, while helping them navigate through the COVID-19 pandemic.

For more information about Shamika, please visit her website: www.bluesunveil.org and follow her on Facebook: www.Facebook.com/Bluesunveil/